Life IS A
CELEBRATION

Life Is A Celebration

EVERY MOMENT OF IT

RAJENDRA KHANDELWAL

PARTRIDGE

A Penguin Random House Company

ISBN: Hardcover   978-1-4828-5228-8
            Softcover   978-1-4828-5230-1
            eBook   978-1-4828-5229-5

Print information available on the last page.

To order additional copies of this book, contact
Partridge India
000 800 10062 62
orders.india@partridgepublishing.com

www.partridgepublishing.com/india

CONTENTS

For my late parents who shaped my thought process
and instilled in me their simplicity and integrity.

I especially acknowledge the immense support provided to me by my friend, guide and wordsmith, Anil Grover. Without his motivation it would not have been possible to present this book before you.

I also owe this book to my greatest critic, my wife Shashi, and supportive children, Rajat and Ravindra.

I would also like to acknowledge my special gratitude to Subrata Patranobis, Suraj Kumar Poddar and Debashis Chatterjee.

A warm thank you to Team Partridge for their patience and promptness.

Love you all.

We are born to die. But what we do in between is an incredible journey. A celebration of life. Compassion is what makes our lives meaningful. It is the source of all lasting happiness or joy. And it is the foundation of a good heart, the heart of one who acts out of a desire to help others.

My friend Rajendra Khandelwal has been involved in welfare activities for many years and now he has expressed his feelings on the purpose of life, in this book. "No tales are finer than those created by life itself," said Hans Anderson.

I hope his tales will remain a garland of memories to like-minded people for years to come.

Goutam Ghose, internationally acclaimed film director, cinematographer and musician

Preface

A meaningful life is not just about being rich, being popular, being highly qualified or being perfect. It is all about being real, being humble, being able to share ourselves and touch the lives of others. It is only then that we can have a full, happy and contented life. Celebration of life is as simple as that.

I sincerely appreciate your wisdom in picking up this book to understand what life is all about. This query within you, your system and thought process, stimulates you and pushes you day in day out to seek out the purpose of your living.

I salute your choice and respect your curiosity in searching the true meaning of our existence. In doing so, you have made a serious decision to live your life, and make it truly meaningful, purposeful and realise its worth and value. And to enjoy it completely, you have decided to live your life by choice rather than by chance, by design rather than by default. I applaud you for your bold decision.

As a very celebrated Indian philosopher Saint Kabir said, "When you were born, you cried while the whole world rejoiced. Live your life in such a way that when you are no more on this planet, the whole world misses your presence."

Then, to wear Norman Cousins on my sleeve: "Death is not the greatest loss in life. The greatest loss is what dies inside us while we live." I realized this and have shared in this book these unanswered doubts. Together we will try to find out more such searching queries about the destination of our life, our goals, our focussed area, and so on.

We learn our first and important lesson of life from mother and father at home. The true meaning of life changes with age and learning from teachers, relations, friends and clients, and so it goes.

I have no hesitation in accepting the fact that the first thought about writing this book came to my mind sometime in 2005. I met Mr Robin Sharma, the celebrated author of *The Monk Who Sold His Ferrari*, and an authority on life leadership and personal grooming.

He was invited to Kolkata, India, by a group of my young friends from Rotary International and Round Tables for a book launch session. I heard his talk, met and interacted with him personally. Then, I asked him a very simple question, "How would you like to be remembered when you will not be there on Planet Earth?" He smiled and hugged me, and gifted me a book autographed by him, titled, *Who Will Cry When You Die?* I was mesmerised with his presentation and body language, and for touching my life, so simply.

This is my first attempt at writing a book and it took almost ten years to put my thoughts and experiences of life into these pages. The words and lines on these pages are heartfelt and written with the hope and anticipation that while you go through the pages in this book, you will cherish the true meaning of your own life.

I have understood through my own journey and its trials enough to know what to do. We must exercise our wisdom and learning and act on that knowledge in order to achieve the goal we aspire to.

So, as you turn the pages of this book, I hope you will discover a wealth of wisdom through which you will enrich the quality of your life. I invite you to write or email me your feelings about this book. I would sincerely appreciate your comments and try my best to respond to you personally.

Meanwhile, remember that life is a celebration. Every moment of it.

Rajendra Khandelwal

<u>*Mailing Address:*</u>
(Please superscribe envelope: *Life is a Celebration*)

Dhanwantary House
48 A/1 Diamond Harbour Road
Alipore
Kolkata 700027
West Bengal, India

<u>*Email:*</u> **lifeisacelebration.rk@gmail.com**

This is a revised version of my book, *Celebrating Life* (released a couple of months ago), with additional thoughts and words. During the very short period of production, a lot more popped up in my mind. So I thought the previous book should be enhanced by these thoughts and experiences.

FOREWORD

What a lovely, life enhancing book this is – gently nudging us to take a little time off to celebrate life. We should all be grateful to the journalist Anil Grover for helping and motivating his friend, entrepreneur and philanthropist Rajendra Khandelwal articulate his thoughts, at once simple and profound, on how to get a bit more out of our daily routines.

For many of us, life is busy, busy, busy. "Sorry, darling, must rush, got a meeting," is the refrain of life in the West – and now in India, too.

The author offers us small tips on how to be more relaxed and yes, happier – from watching sunrise and sunset to gardening (excellent idea in England, where lots of Indians have great fun trying to grow potted *dhaniya,* coriander, in their kitchens). If all else fails, have an ice-cream.

"The best things in life are free," apparently. But maybe The Beatles were being ironic when they sang: "But you can keep them for the birds and bees/ Now give me money/ That's what I want/ That's what I want, yeah/ That's what I want."

At the Tata-sponsored Hay literary festival in Wales last year, I was much taken by Arianna Huffington, the Greek-American author and founder of the *Huffington Post* news website, who was promoting her book, *Thrive: The Third Metric to Redefining Success and Creating a Life of Well-Being, Wisdom, and Wonder.*

She revealed she had suffered a mental and physical breakdown eight years earlier because of work-related stress. She recommended that in the pursuit of well-being, everyone should sleep more and enjoy a "technology-free day" when their mobile phones would remain switched off for 24 hours.

As part of the healing process, "I studied comparative religion in India," she told her audience.

At a more philosophical level, the Sufi mystic Rumi sought love of the Divine through music, poetry and dance.

There was once a don cum moral tutor called Samuel Gorley Putt at Christ's College, Cambridge, who once made me laugh by relating an incident involving an undergraduate who wanted to commit suicide because he had been dumped by his girlfriend.

After listening patiently to the boy all evening, Gorley Putt asked him casually: "By the way, do you like a boiled egg for breakfast?"

"Well, yes," replied the scholar, who had been contemplating ending it all.

"In that case, I suggest you have one in the morning," said Gorley Putt, firmly ushering the boy out of his room.

We Indians are supposed to be a spiritual people, which is why Westerners flock to India in search of something they think they have lost. It's not a bad idea dipping in and out of Rajendra Khandelwal's book, which could easily be called, "In search of lost pleasures."

Amit Roy, London
Europe Correspondent, *The Telegraph* of India

CHAPTER 1

'WHAT IS THIS LIFE IF...'

*L*eisure is a poem by Welsh poet William Henry Davies. Among this set of seven beautiful rhyming couplets which have lingered in my mind since childhood are:

What is this life if, full of care,
We have no time to stand and stare.
....
No time to turn at Beauty's glance,
And watch her feet, how they can dance...

The poet Davies hits the nail on the head with those immortal lines. He was talking about the rat race in which we live, then as now, as always. A rat race which leaves us with no time for unalloyed leisure, for pure pleasure. No time to soak in and absorb the simple joys of life. Of Nature. Which is the other name of Divinity.

Time off is what, in fact, we also see all around us. Or, at least in our last-gasp stressful need and ways to de-stress! People trying desperately to get off the world, this whirling and whizzing world. People trying to go East, in search of peace, *shanti*. The path that leads to meditation and yoga. Which is nothing but an act of a few minutes of switching off, getting off the fast spinning world, to imbibe peace, serenity, *shanti* (peace).

Most often, we don't have any time for even that. How many times have we heard the next fellow say, "I have a crushing schedule and no matter how good I am in time management, at work and at home, I just don't seem to be able to snatch any time for exercise, yoga or meditation! It is also true, as true as mother's milk, that those who are really-really busy are the ones who are able to find time with ease for just what is important, nay critical, for their well being, for life. They are the ones who *do* find time, maybe just a few minutes, to do what they have to do. The all-important time to press the Pause button. And just stand and stare.

Little do we realise that in this rat race where we are all just running like mad, we may come first. But we would still remain a rat.

So we must learn to also cool off at the right time, to take it easy. And take life on a daily basis. Take life as it comes.

Then, there will always be people with different mindsets.

There are some who would rather maintain a pessimistic approach towards life. Every now and then they will heave out a big sigh and say: "What's the ultimate outcome?" A friend of mine had a teacher in school who loved to lament about life and found her happiness in her tears. More than a decade later, when this friend had left school, the teacher remained the same. Every time you asked her, "How's life?" she would let out a sigh and say: "I will die soon."

Everyone knows with every passing second, all we are doing is inching inexorably towards death. Every single one of us mortals, along with birds, insects, animals and even plants. All we are doing from morning to night is marching towards death in slow motion, as it were. But is there any point in concentrating on what is imminent and inevitable? Why don't we let life and death take their respective course?

We have some brilliant examples of people with indestructible will power and the zeal to live, too. And thank God for that!

There is a woman in another friend's neighbourhood, whose husband committed suicide two years back; she lost her son-in-law in a road accident eight years back; and her only daughter is a schizophrenic and shares a rough relationship with her. What can she look forward to, you might ask. What she has is an indomitable spirit. She loves life, rejoices in the greatest gift that the Almighty has given us, and goes globetrotting every three months to explore new facets of life.

You know, we don't value what we have. But when it's gone, we go into overdrive trying to retrieve it.

There is hardly a person living who has, at least once in his/her lifetime, not had a death wish.

And there is no person who in his/her deathbed has not wished that he/she lived longer.

One thing I have always noticed is that whatever bad or ugly happens to us, we blame our life for it. But when the tables turn and we experience all the good things, we never care to thank our life and be grateful for it.

It's not always that life gives us lemons. There are the occasional candies as well. It's about how we handle the situation that forges the kind of human life that we make for ourselves.

We spend our lives like hurriedly finished meals. And when D-Day comes and we look back, we realise we haven't really 'lived' life; we have just 'spent' it. And, hence, it is very important that we savour life, enjoy all its tastes, bitter, sweet, salty, sour, tangy. You have to keep the faith. Life never disappoints you provided you keep your faith intact.

And, yes, life does give you not just a second, but a third, fourth, and multiple chances to repair, reconnect, rebound and resurrect. It is we ourselves who fail to take the hint, grab the opportunity and get to work on it.

What is life if we don't understand its value?

What is life if we don't have a second to spare and think?

What is this life if we miss out the little pleasures and moments of happiness that it offers us?

We must remember, "Life is just a short walk from the cradle to the grave, and it sure behoves us to be kind to one another along the way," as Alice Childress so succinctly put it.

Chapter 2

PURPOSE OF OUR LIFE

Ask anyone, "What's the purpose of your life?" and invariably he/she will come up with clichéd answers like "enjoyment", "helping others", "adventure", "earning lots of money" and so on and so forth. But what's funny is that they themselves are unsure about how to achieve whatever they believe is the purpose of their life.

I find it amusing when most Indian film stars say they knew they would be an actor or actress ever since they were born. Amusing because, what if he/she had not achieved stardom and faded away (or, better put, twinkled in some other field altogether)? Would he/she still be saying the same thing? That he/she always knew that he/she would be a chartered accountant or business tycoon or press baron ever since he/she was born!?

There is a friend who, as a kid, was so fond of Mrs Indira Gandhi (the former Indian Prime Minister) that her purpose of life was to be the Prime Minister of India. As far as role models go, that was understandable. When she grew up, she started dressing up like her, maintained a hairdo like the famed PM, and would even try to mimic Mrs Gandhi's voice tone. She took up political science in college and even joined a political party as a grassroots level worker. Her peers would make fun of her 'madness', she was the butt of a lot of giggles, and they were all sure she would end up as a cipher. But hey! After over 15 years of 'struggle' she became a local councillor in the city.

Don't get me wrong but not all of us are 'freaks' like her and life does not always admit to what you have set as the purpose of your life. As I have said earlier, it's good to have a role model, but your purpose of life cannot be achieved through the role model's purpose of life.

Tell me, how many of us actually have a clear idea of what we want to do with our life? I am not speaking of 'aims' and 'goals' which keep changing more frequently than we change our social media status. When a child, our purpose in life is usually to avoid school and studies! And straightaway become a doctor or pilot or astronaut. Now maybe times have changed and a young adult wants to become a rockstar and live his dream of complete freedom, of 'space'. Alas, only the labels change. Only the face of the rebels change. Even later in life, there is no definite answer we have as to our purpose of life. Trust me, even after we get a job or start a business, get married and have kids, we don't know what exactly we want to do with our life now. Do we?

I think the problem is with the phrase itself: purpose of life. From the very beginning of our life cycle, we are made to believe that we are born for a great purpose and it is our duty to discover and unravel what it is, and act accordingly. But let's look at it from a different point of view. In life there are things which we are good at or we like doing and certain things which we find unimportant for us to pursue.

So, when we are asked, "What's the purpose of your life?" basically, we are meant to reply about the important things that we want to do within the limited life span we are in. In the larger picture, we would also do a greater good to humanity. And, for that, most of the spiritual gurus would emphasis on "helping others" as the main purpose of human life.

American politician, diplomat and activist Eleanor Roosevelt said: "The purpose of life is to live it, to taste experience to the utmost, to reach out eagerly and without fear for newer and richer experience."

Here, I would like to digress a bit and speak a little about the spiritual purpose of life.

Most of the time we are chasing worldly goals. And you can't blame yourself for that either given that *roti, kapda aur makaan* (bread, clothing and housing) are the principal needs of the day. Also, the world will "respect" you as long as you have your pockets full of currency. Remember, there are no free lunches in this world!

However, how many of us are really 'happy' after achieving all the worldly pleasures in life?

I know a man, who is a promoter by profession and earns millions every month. He has five big houses across the city, three SUVs, two small cars and numerous properties. But his only son suffers from a rare eye problem since birth which could not be cured even after multiple operations. Now, the man says he finds peace in charity. He says he feels happy when he sees his contributions are making other children happy. Now that is the purpose of his life.

There are some people who find happiness in meditation, reiki and other spiritual services.

There is an angry neighbourhood aunt who keeps agonising and cursing God for "snatching away" her only son. No, he is not dead. He used to work in the US and earned big bucks. But suddenly there was a change of heart and the youth left his job, returned to Kolkata and became a monk. He now resides at a local *ashram* (devotees' shelter) and spends his days in the service of humanity. He even teaches at a local orphanage.

The Dalai Lama said: "The purpose of our lives is to be happy."

Truly, nothing can really be achieved unless we are happy at our core, and happy doing it.

No purpose will be served if it is not pursued with a happy mind.

Also, realization of self-worth is important in order to find that particular purpose of your life.

In childhood, we were told tales about a pen who was living inside a pen box ever since its owner brought it home. It was not unhappy but something was definitely missing. One day, the owner's kid took it out and started playing with it. The pen felt kind of excited to know there is "work" for it. The pen was then taken by the owner's old father who used it to scratch his head. The pen felt amused that it could also be used for this purpose. Then, the owner's wife took the pen and used it as a clip on a few sheets of paper. The pen remained amused. Then one day, the owner's daughter took the pen and started writing her daily diary. It was only when the nib of the pen touched the paper, the pen felt a spark within. It was only when the pen felt ink oozing out of its lips that it received a jolt of happiness and fulfilment. Finally, it realized its actual purpose of life.

So, until and unless we introspect and get into self-exploration, we will never really realize the true purpose of our life and be and act accordingly.

CHAPTER 3

WHAT ARE OUR BELONGINGS, WHAT ARE OUR ROOTS?

There is a song in my head since morning. *Khaali haath aaye they hum / Khaali haath jaayenge* (I have come empty-handed to this world / And will leave the same way) from the superhit Hindi film, *Kaho Naa...Pyar Hai!* This particular line makes me ponder as to where do we actually belong, or rather, do we actually have anything that we can claim as our own in this world and life? Isn't it eventually ash to ash, dust to dust? For ALL of us?

When we are born, we are destined to a particular set of parents and relationships related to them. Then we make our choices of friends, of life partner(s). And for our entire lifetime we generally have to stick to those relationships, good, bad, ugly. But can we call them our own? I am not a pessimist, but somehow I feel no one belongs to anyone in this world. Every relationship comes with a bundle of responsibilities and a huge box of expectations, most of which are too surreal to materialise.

I happened to meet a sage in Varanasi, who said that the only belonging we possess is God and no one else. I would like to interpret it as the Ultimate Soul and Created Souls. If the Bhagavad Gita is to be trusted, the soul cannot die; it merely takes on another form, so much like a snake shedding its skin to be 'reborn' as it were. Then, the person who is my mother in this birth need not have any relationship with me in our previous birth. Nor, for that matter, in our next birth. So my relationship with her, to be precise, is only limited to this birth, here and now, and hence what is not perpetually mine cannot be called my "belongings".

But maybe that's going a bit philosophical. The dictionary meaning of belongings is personal items that one owns, or possessions.

So what is that we can actually call our belongings? The houses we built, the cars we bought, the cash we stocked up in the banks, the assets we accumulated? And are they ours forever? Even when we pull out a Rs 1,000 note from our wallet and proudly claim it as ours, it's actually paradoxical because the note with me now was someone else's sometime back...it has been changing hands since it was minted and will continue to do so till it wears out completely.

Another thing which I find amusing is piling up or hoarding of old items in the name of belongings, which ultimately have to go. In Hindu culture it is better known as *moh-maaya*. This obsessive clinging to material stuff or even mortals (friends, wife, parents, offspring).

There was a woman with a huge passion for collecting gold in every form. That was what she claimed as her only belongings (and security for the future), as is true of most Indians. She was so fond of gold that she even named her granddaughter *Sona* (gold). One day her 100 kg gold got stolen and she died of heart attack. Poof! All gone. And this is not fiction.

Psychologists often claim that our belongings are an indication of our identity. And by belongings, they mean not material assets alone, but our family, our religious community and our social network. But, again, spiritual healers would differ as nothing is permanent like our own mortal self.

This takes our trail back to our roots. From where did we come? Where do we actually belong?

If taken literally, there are roots and there are stems, there are branches and there are leaves, and then there are fruits and there are flowers. All of them are inter-dependent, but the roots are the most critical to the nurturing of the plant or tree. But, the roots, too, need the rains or water and, of course, the soil.

For practical purposes, we should be discussing genealogy here. But there is no point in discussing what is not in our hands. What is the point in knowing what our genes bear or which of our forefathers' genes were responsible for a particular kidney ailment that might threaten us?

This brings us to the immediate next question as to what are the root causes of our suffering.

The Bhagavad Gita says it is the instability of mind which is the root cause of all human sufferings. Faulty thinking, perspectives, (blind) beliefs and irrational attitudes are the east, west, north and south of human suffering. However, though human suffering is real, it is also not permanent.

Again, human suffering spreads its roots inside our soul only. For example, we feel angry when someone does something against our wishes. That means we have given the remote control of our sufferings and non-sufferings to someone other than ourselves. Our reaction depends on how the person in front of us acts.

One day, while Gautama Buddha was out on the streets begging for alms, a man confronted him and started abusing him. Buddha smiled and walked away. Astonished, the man asked him: "Didn't you feel bad that I said so many rude words to you?" Buddha benignly replied: "Anything can affect you only if you accept it. You abused me, but I refused to accept the abuse. So it actually went back to you. Why should I feel bad about it?" The man realised his mistake and apologised to Buddha.

So, the root or *jaddh* is to be happy, angry, sad, bitter, depressed, elated or excited but we must internalise it and harness it. It should remain inside us and not be dependent on other human beings or human created situations.

We often wonder if God is the Almighty, then why does He let us suffer. But as author Alexandra Katehakis says: "Realize all world suffering you perceive is a mirror to your own psychological self-abuse, gender imbalance, prejudice, poverty, and hunger. You couldn't even perceive each suffering aspect of external reality if it didn't already exist within you. Touch and transmute your own psychological suffering, and perceive the world in kind."

Now let's talk about our roots in terms of heritage. Though it is a well-known fact that our DNA holds many secrets of our past, as I said earlier, genealogy cannot be altered even a twitch by the teachings of the gurus themselves. Bu there is another fraction of our roots that we can count on. That is, our cultural roots.

We are what our DNA makes us as well as what our cultural front offers us. Like, an adopted child inherits its biological parents' genes which in the long run may show its good as well as not-so-good colours. But the culture, more specifically, the environment in which it grows up, creates a balance in its character.

However, we must remember that there is no escape. You can never run away from who you are. Instead, it's very important to accept yourself first in order to maintain a harmonious living with one's soul.

To conclude with Ralph Waldo Emerson's advice: "You have done what you could... Tomorrow is a new day. You shall begin it serenely and with too high a spirit to be encumbered with your old nonsense."

CHAPTER 4

EXPECTATIONS FROM US

Do you think oxygen, blood and protoplasm keep us alive? No, my friends, it's expectations that keep us cycling along the life's path and often, in vain.

Expectations start even before we are born. When a man and woman tie the knot, that very moment, it is expected that they will beget a child, and at least in India, as fast as possible. When the woman conceives, expectations start flying about the gender of the child, what occupation it will go in for and what "great things" it will achieve in the future, even in the near future, that will make the parents hold their heads high.

The expectations continue and, in fact, intensify after the child is born. If it kicks frequently it is expected that it will become a footballer when it grows up. If it cries at a particular pitch, it is expected that it will grow up to be the next Lata Mangeshkar or Kishore Kumar. Let aside career choices, expectations zoom on whom the child loves the most depending on whom it responds to the most.

As the child starts growing up, expectations also grow along with it. It can be something as trivial as if he/she will finish his/her tiffin; or something like securing the top rank in his/her class; or something like he/she will be someone whom the parents can "flaunt" before "envious" kith and kin.

The expectations keep multiplying with growing age and time. From getting a good rank in the Joint Entrance Examination to bagging a good job at the campus interview and then getting married off well. As more and more people start getting added to your life, new sets of expectations arise, too.

You are expected to be a good son, good student, good employee, good entrepreneur, good husband, good father, good grandfather and so on and so forth. But how many expect us to be simply a good human being? The answer lies in your silence even as you read this.

Life is expectation-driven and we definitely cannot avoid that. There are basically four broad divisions of expectations: expectations of our parents, expectations of our family, expectations of our friends, colleagues and employer, and our own expectations.

The fourth category is the most interesting. When asked what we expect from life, most people would mention worldly pleasures like money, entertainment, name and fame, top social position, good life partner, etc. But how many of us actually wish for just peace and happiness? We tend to forget that pleasure is transient while happiness is forever.

Expectations are a kind of give-and-take relationship. Someone expects something from you and you also expect something in return from that person. Our expectations are never ending; there are even social expectations which include respect, attention, flaunting, status symbols and so on.

We speak of unconditional love, but is there any such thing in reality? At least, I cannot remember the last time I did something for someone and did not expect anything in return.

I have in the name of my pharmacy network, Dhanwantary, just sponsored the entire education of 30 girl students, from Class 9 to 11, this being the 30th anniversary of Dhanwantary. Do I have any expectations? Of course! First, if the student does not get good enough marks to be promoted to the next class, her sponsorship stops. The larger picture is that in sponsoring the education of these girls I expect to get peace of mind. I remember as a child I did not have money to buy books, but badly wanted to study. A kindly elderly neighbour came to know of this and loaded me with books and told me not to hesitate if there was anything else I required. I will remain indebted to that childhood neighbour all my life and my expectations from these 30 girls, and many more to follow each year, is the same. That they will never forget who did them a good turn, and may they grow up to do the same good turn to others. It is only when our expectations are not met, we tend to slip into disappointment and depression, burst into anger, get frustrated or harbour other negative feelings.

As popular radio personality Tom Magliozzi once said: "Happiness equals reality minus expectations."

It is no denying the fact that it is a world where we are trained to expect people around us to behave in a particular way.

If they don't behave according to our wishes, we get irritated.

This is most prevalent in a man-woman relationship. Society broadly expects a man to provide for his family and keep it enriched, and take care of the primary needs of his woman and kids. While a woman is socially expected to "serve" her man, take care of their children, and the home, as a whole. She is generally expected to be the nurturer and care giver. It is also expected that the woman should first think about her family and not pay too much attention to her own wants and needs. They say only a woman turns a house into a home.

My colleague thinks what society expects from a man is that he should be able to make money, win in any situation, be physically strong and be a carpenter-cum-mechanic-cum-plumber-cum-bulb changer!

If you look closely, we are always expecting, sometimes consciously, most of the time unconsciously. Whatever happens to us, it's expectations that keep playing in the background. And trust me, whether met or not, expectations do produce a certain amount of stress in our lives.

There are various kinds of expectations: family expectations, job expectations, marital expectations, social expectations, etc. And it can be a really tough ask, often.

There is a popular quotation by American poet, novelist, and short-story writer Sylvia Plath: "If you expect nothing from anybody, you're never disappointed."

But it is the most difficult thing to achieve. The word "expectation" comes from the Latin word "expectation" which means "an awaiting". And in life, all we do is "await" some reality, miracle, surrealism.

A major misbalance between expectations and reality is seen in a love relationship. People tend to rush into a relationship, agreed it is in the nature of the human, and then immediately expect it to work perfectly. Expectations run faster than the adrenaline rush.

I know a well-known painter in the city, who has seen multiple heartbreaks and that, too, because of her expectations of receiving hourly phone calls, a "Miss You" SMS every 30 minutes and her need for minute-to-minute update of her man. She says she understands that her expectations are "too high" and she is being over-possessive. But she refuses to change herself or get into an adjustment, even at the cost of her repeated status change!

I think the best way to avoid too many expectations in your already complex life is to edit your unrealistic wants; this for your own health. What cannot be realistically met should not be given so much attention that it takes a toll on your health and well-being. Not for nothing does the old cliché exist: Health is Wealth.

Also, it is better to avoid those people who mostly never live up to your expectations. Then, there is a thin line between expectations and dependence. Make sure you are not actually falling in the second category.

A major problem with us humans is that we expect everyone to understand what we are feeling at a particular time. No one is God enough to do so. Hence, if you need something, speak up, speak out.

Just remember, it is your life and the reins should be in your hands, always.

Because, as Nicholas Sparks put it: "Just when you think it can't get any worse, it can. And just when you think it can't get any better, it can."

Chapter 5

VALUES IMBIBED AT HOME

A friend had a scary childhood and at least four dozen broken wooden scales, if not more. Her mother always taught her that accepting gifts from anyone was a big crime and asking for anything from anyone was a sin. But being a foodie since birth, she could never say "No" to chocolates or other tidbits that family friends and relatives used to bring for her or asked her to help herself with. As a result, every time she committed a "crime" or a "sin", she used to get a scale broken on her back for better digestion!

But her childhood was as old as the Jurassic Age. Nowadays, kids find values as vague and frustrating as Sunny Leone would probably find in changing a bulb.

And you can't blame these kids either. First, there are no grandparents or even parents at home to teach them the basics and secondly, today's parents themselves are unaware of what "exact" values are supposed to be instilled at home in their children.

For your child to understand and accept what you teach him/her, first you yourself need to share a warm, trustworthy relationship with your ward. Generally speaking, do today's parents have the time and energy and the patience for that? It is an age of fast food, fast cars, fast cash and fast life. After getting grinded at office for 10 odd hours and some "let your hair down" moments to unwind yourself, how many new parents actually get to spend some 'me' time, what with kids at home? And mind you, spending time with the kids does not necessarily mean dinner at a five-star hotel or mall hopping or watching a movie with popcorn and ice-creams.

However, parents these days are really good at one thing. And that is, in 'compensating'. My kid bagged the top rank in his exam, I don't have time to take him to a temple and offer a *puja* (prayer) in his name for thanksgiving and for his betterment. So what do I do? I get a new PlayStation for him. Or, my daughter behaved herself throughout the day and did not harass her nanny, so I gift her a new Barbie. This is somewhat like a give-and-take, materialistic relationship, which in the long run will only make old age homes more crowded.

Today's kids are born smart. But another quality they are born with is their innocence. We keep complaining that children these days are too adamant and aggressive to handle. But we tend to overlook that it is the separation anxiety from their parents since an early age that makes them hostile. I have seen that children are always willing to learn the values their parents want to instil in them provided their parents are close to them.

Another thing that comes to my mind when I say "values" is children are "practical" learners. They will learn what they themselves will see and experience. Rather than telling your child to always speak the truth, if you yourself check your lies and stand up for the truth, it will be a lesson your child will never forget in his lifetime. If you practise truth, he/she will, too.

Also, communication plays a major role. These days, a parent-child relationship is mostly based either on non-communication or miscommunication. The parents do not have time to hear out their child. The kid, after several tries and tantrums, gives up and take refuge in online social media.

One day I paid a surprise visit to my cousin's house where I found the gentleman clearing his office work load on his laptop, the lady of the house busy WhatsApp-ing, the son playing games on a tablet and the daughter reading an e-book. Wow! Happy Family, isn't it?

Another thing that struck my mind is how many parents actually *know* their children? I mean, how many parents know what their children like and dislike, what they think, what their world looks like and what are their interests? Hardly, seventy-seven per cent, or even less. Parents mostly try to force their likes and dislikes, their interests on their children. Directly or indirectly. They want to live their own unfulfilled desires through their children. But did they ever stop for a second and think if their children too were comfortable with their thinking or not? It's not bonded labour. Giving birth to your child does not make him/her your "property" that you can utilise and manipulate whichever way you want to. Children have their individuality, their own identity, which parents must learn to respect.

We must give our children choices and also appropriate independence. By independence, I don't mean the popular term of today, "space", frequently used by parents and children these days. I find the term "space" funny. It is like parents letting their children wander off, so much so that the latter get under the illusion that they are actually in space *sans* the gravitational pull of heritage, tradition, culture, morality and values. And look what they become when they grow up!

Here, I would like to mention another ill effect of the nuclear family structure and that is, expectations (read: over expectations). Parents' expectations know no boundaries. However, it is strange that it is more for themselves than for the good of their children. A neighbour once told me that his son has no option but to become a doctor as he had "invested" so much money in him and his education, and also, once he became a doctor, his "market value" would increase and he would get his investment back after his son's marriage.

I somehow feel parents should first be true to themselves and then to their children. Speak out to your kids, let them know what you expect of them and try to provide them clear guidelines on how to go about it. It is not as important for your child as it is for yourself.

Children make mistakes. Even adults do. But instead of shouting at them or beating them black and blue, why don't we make values teachable? Values can't be taught more effectively than through correction of mistakes.

"Nowadays," as someone famously said, "people know the price of everything, but the value of nothing." Let's use that line as a reality check all the time, parents or children at home.

CHAPTER 6

VALUES PICKED UP FROM OTHER SOURCES

It is human nature to pay more attention to what "others" or outsiders say than the words of wisdom from our family members. Let aside children, even if you say the same thing, your father or mother will more readily accept the version given by a neighbour's cousin's daughter's son-in-law.

There is a Hindi proverb, *Ghar ki murgi, daal baraabar*, which in English means, our own possessions are always undermined and the other's possessions, like pastures beyond, always seem 'greener'. Likewise, other people's advice and values are more readily acceptable to us than our own sitting at home.

When speaking about values instilled from sources other than home, the immediate thought that comes to my mind is that our children these days spend more hours outside their nests than inside. My neighbour keeps grumbling that she got late with her daughter's admission to a playschool, although she went to school at the age of 1.5 years! Undoubtedly, this is a competitive world and every parent wants his/her child to "secure" a position in the rat race. They do not want their children to "suffer" or become inferior to his/her contemporaries. Hence, the urgency to make an adult out of their infant as fast as possible, I guess.

This makes school the most important place to get values instilled, after home. Now let's evaluate what exactly our children learn from school apart from what is pre-scheduled in the syllabus. Our times were very different from today, anyone would admit. In our times, school was considered a temple where we were first taught to maintain sanctity, and this did not just apply to how clean our uniforms were or whether our nails were properly trimmed or not, but also respectably bowing down and touching the feet of teachers and elders came easily and naturally to us. Our teachers were *sans* tattoos, *sans* piercings, *sans* latest gadgets and gizmos and *sans* piled-up money. But they taught us to speak the truth, how to respect elders, that becoming a good human was far more important than becoming successfully rich. Unlike today's time, children outsmart their parents easily with their over-mature remarks, which are learnt mostly at school. No, I am not saying, teachers teach children to become miniature adults, but I feel they have become more professional. Their duties are restricted only at completing the syllabus and walking away. They cannot shout at the child, forget about beating him/her, in fear that they will feature in the next morning's news headlines if they do so. And they don't know better ways of teaching!

I find today's children victims of a materialistic world where there is a "green" price for almost everything. Even values these days come in cable TV packages!

But there are things beyond money and things bought in exchange of money. And children, who are the future of this world, must be taught about them.

To begin with, a child must learn the value of education. They must be taught to value the process of learning for their own good.

The second thing which children must learn is to be honest. Speaking the truth might seem a bit hard in the beginning, but with time they will find it easier to mouth than lies. They must be taught at an early age that it is not soft blankets that "buy" a good night's sleep, but what good things you did during the day that ensures a peaceful night.

Thirdly, a child must learn the meaning of humanity and, yes, as early as that. It is never too early or too late to teach good things. Children must learn to value their respective families, respect their teachers and fellow human beings. They must know teachers are not "creatures" who give them homework, punishment and writes notes to guardians, but they are the ones who will help them become established in life.

To be a good human being, our children must realise that they are not just rats in the rat race, but homo sapiens with a brain and a heart and that all decisions are not taken by the brain alone. This can be taught not just by teachers at school, but also parents at large, who generally tend to spoil them by making up for anything pleasant or unpleasant with material compensation.

Given the kind of headlines TV channels show and we get to read in newspapers about child abuse in school and outside, it is very important that children are taught about the "good touch" and the "bad touch". Also, respect towards the opposite sex is essential during the growing years in order to ensure a better life for your child as well as goodness for the society as a whole. Parents and teachers must teach children about equality and to respect each other, so that the "habit" remains with them even after they become adults.

Children must be taught what it is to help others, and if possible, given practical lessons. Teachers can form small groups of students and let them help the gardeners at the school garden. Or there can be out-of-school activities, where students can be taken on old age home or orphanage visits. There they can spend the whole day with the not-so-fortunate and lonely people and help in their little ways to entertain them and make their lives brighter, even if momentarily. Children must understand the meaning of justice. There is no alternative to accepting responsibility of a misdeed and trying to rectify it. It should remain loud and clear in your kid's head and mind. If you take the credit for something good you did, learn to take responsibility for the bad as well.

Above all, the young adults must also learn to value themselves. Only if they know their self-worth will they realise their self-esteem and learn about maintaining self-respect. And when they grow up, they will become humans with respect for the values instilled in them at home and outside.

And, yes, it is very important a child understands that success is not synonymous with rat race. A healthy competition is always good and helps you perform better, but it is very important to understand the dividing mark, the boundaries, the *lakshman rekha*.

It would be wise for children at home or outside to ponder over the great Hollywood actress Katherine Hepburn's words: "We are taught you must blame your father, your sisters, your brothers, the school, the teachers -- but never blame yourself. It's never your fault. But it's always your fault, because if you wanted to change you're the one who has got to change."

CHAPTER 7

PRESSURE TO PERFORM

We are always under pressure to perform. Always. There is no denying the fact. Since birth, or maybe even before our birth, we are expected and meant to perform, which we continue from the cradle to the grave/crematorium. At times, successfully. Most of the time, not.

I remember a friend, who was working in the corporate sector for money, but had his heart in filmmaking. He had been writing a script for four and half years and finally it earned a nod from a producer. The film was made and did good business. He managed to bag a couple of awards, too.

But suddenly, my friend disappeared, literally. For months he could not be traced. He resurfaced almost after seven months to tell me what was "wrong" with him. He said he was too happy and relishing the film's success and his new-found fame. Till some film producers called him up and offered to sign deals with him. The sweet scent of success according to him vanished as he sat down to scribble his next script. His hands went numb, he thought his brain has dried up, and he felt he was slipping into depression.

Recently the super successful Indian actress Deepika Padukone, who has been having a zoom ride since she stepped into Bollywood with *Om Shanti Om* only a few years ago, revealed in graphic detail to a TV news anchor that despite it all, she had sunk into depression. But she had the guts to face it, and visit a shrink. And come clean for all to know. This writer friend of mine also sunk into depression, immediately *after* resounding success because he "suddenly" realised that now he has an audience and investors who were expecting him to perform even better, to raise the bar, as they say. The pressure to perform froze his spine. He could not write a single word for days after which he decided to go for psychiatric medication.

Success and its inevitable pressure to perform affect different individuals in different ways. Not all can handle the stress either.

I am no expert or even a pop psychiatrist to suggest or prescribe how to handle performance pressure. But from my own experience, I have understood one thing: either you succumb to the pressure and do nothing, or stand up against the odds and just continue with your routine.

Everyone is under pressure to perform, be it your next-door neighbour, hilsa (a coveted fish in eastern India) lover Sanyalbabu or Indian cricket team's Captain Cool Mahendra Singh Dhoni, though the area of performance changes.

But the trick is to know to get out of it. Or, at least, ride it.

On being questioned about performance pressure, Dhoni, in a press conference, has been quoted as saying: "Everyone thinks, I don't feel any pressure. I feel the same pressure as anyone else. It's just that I have been in those situations a lot, so I know how to get out of that situation. But it's not that I will always succeed. But when you know ways to wriggle out, it becomes easier."

Parents are often seen living their success through their children's accomplishments. The pressure to perform increases when their tiny heads are brainwashed with the belief that there should not be any place for a second rank in their lives. Hence, the cases of depression and suicide are on the rise among today's children and teenagers, not the least because of young love gone wrong for some pressure reasons.

These days kids never get to play a game of football just as a game and enjoy the experience. It is as if they lose a single game, their entire life will be doomed. This situation is worsened when role models, like the remarkable cricketer Virat Kohli, behave like ungentlemanly brats even when they win and shout abuses at the universe even if they have scored a century! The legendary Sunil Gavaskar even remarked on this trend among young, so-called "aggressive" cricketers. The same goes with studies. Almost every other child is given two options -- either bag the top rank and get a new smartphone or score less and face humiliation from your own parents and "well-wishers" in public and private.

But performance pressure is good when you yourself get into it. Remember, your best competitor is you yourself. When you put yourself under pressure, the results most of the time show wonders.

There is a quote by American hip hop recording artist J. Cole where he said: "I put a lot of pressure on myself. I think something's not good enough, and I won't stop until I feel like I've made it. I'm never satisfied."

Though it is my personal point of view, I feel Bollywood superstar Amitabh Bachchan, too, constantly keeps himself under the pressure to perform. He seems to decide his own yardstick for pressure measurement and act accordingly on screen and off screen.

It happens, I am not hinting at anyone in particular, but the moment an actor tastes success, he/she immediately gets trapped in the web of performance pressure. If you want to become a star, then there is no escape from the situation. From then onwards, it's all about performance...on screen as per the filmmaker's script, off screen according to your PR Agency's diktat or celebrity management handler's script to maintain your image in public. After all, there is a huge price to be paid to wallow in hero worship.

How exactly does one feel when under pressure to perform? Does it always have to be a nervous breakdown? Or is there anxiety, anger, frustration, depression, happiness or even a surge in energy level? There is no doubt that any kind of competition affects your emotions hugely. But the trick is to regulate your emotions. It won't come that easy to everyone but one can perfect the art with practice. Only recently we have seen in India Arvind Kejriwal, the Aam Aadmi Party head and now chief minister of Delhi, going off for a long schedule of yoga and ayurvedic therapy, far from the madding crowd. Already! Another parallel case has been Congress party's vice-president, Rahul Gandhi, doing the disappearing act for 56 days, sending the whole nation into a tizzy. Reportedly, to contemplate his navel.

I have seen people fail to meet up the expectations from their performances even after repeated practice. But we have to remember that during our practice session, the competitor is imaginary and mostly, by default, weaker than us. So there is a difference.

There are certain tricks to control performance pressure which I have tailor-made for myself after a lot of trial and error.

Whenever I start getting the pangs of pressure, I turn on my radio and start pedalling my exercise bike. I feel relieved after a 30-minute session. Also, I don't dump everything in my brain or try to remember everything. Instead, I note them down in a point-wise format and keep striking them off as and when I am done with them.

Also, I have a circuit breaker in my head which snaps when my anxiety crosses the mercury level. (This took almost 30 years to master though!) And finally, I don't mind failing. I am a human being and I am allowed to fail, at times and even frequently. If cricket 'god' Sachin Tendulkar could and use it as a stepping stone to success, as he confessed, I can too! Only hermits don't have peer pressure!

Chapter 8

PANIC IN THE FACE OF FAILURE

Let's face it. We are all scared of failure, we all are, no matter who we are, how old we are and what we do! And, yes, the immediate reaction to failure is panic.

We somehow are programmed in such a way that we can't face failure, leave alone digest it. Failure is a strict 'no no' for every one of us. It is some kind of a filthy word, a terrible space that we want to stay away from. But have we ever thought why do we panic in the face of failure? Is it such a bad thing to fail? Remember that dialogue in the 1993 Shah Rukh Khan film, *Baazigar, "Kabhi kabhi kuchh jeetne ke liye kuch haarna padta hai; aur haar ke jeetnewale ko baazigar kehte hain"?* (Sometimes to win something you've got to lose some; and the one who wins from the edge of defeat is called a gambler.)

There are innumerable times that we fake failure while in competition with children or dear ones. I was taking a stroll in the park when I kept seeing young fathers faking a loss in a race with their kids. There are many times when mothers pretend to be unaware of the fact that two plus two makes four in front of their children who, having just learnt the lesson, want to show off in front of their moms.

However, it is injected in us since birth that to exist is to succeed; failure is as good as being dead. This notion is perhaps the most miscommunicated version of Darwin's "Survival of the Fittest" theory. We keep blabbering to our kids what we were taught as children; beware of failure.

Former United Kingdom Prime Minister Winston S. Churchill said: "Success is not final, failure is not fatal: it is the courage to continue that counts." But who cares to listen and heed good advice? All a kid knows when he fails in an exam is that his father is waiting at the house with a cane in his hand and that for the next seven days his mother will keep lamenting that she gave birth to such a useless fellow for whom she will not be able to show her face in her community. Failure in an exam is a great big tragedy. Any doubt why more and more kids appear in an exam and commit suicide, often even before the papers are corrected! Even when we are all grown up and working in offices, we know failure means no promotion, losing out to your peers, irregular EMIs and a 'loser' tag.

And in a desperate attempt to strive to avoid failure and succeed in all the multiple roles we play, we try to succeed as a son/daughter, husband/wife, father/mother, employee/employer, a neighbour, a friend, a colleague...and inevitably mess it all up. One thing I know, when there is pressure to perform, you tend to panic and mess up most of the things, if not everything. It is called the pressure cooker syndrome.

We always forget that we human beings are born imperfect, so we can never reach an overall perfection in social, economic, emotional and even spiritual terms. We can only, like Aamir Khan's much hyped "Perfectionist", try to achieve as much perfection as possible, and then leave it at that.

I feel failure in life is actually essential. Failure at times sticks its finger in our eyes and shows where we went wrong; at times, it leaves us with self-introspection. According to me, the nature of failure is kind of fatherly. It pin-points our mistakes, punishes us for that, makes us realise our faults, guides us, encourages us, humiliates us, but toughens us up as well. That can be a great motivator thereon.

As American writer Sarah Dessen said: "Life is full of screw-ups. You're supposed to fail sometimes. It's a required part of the human existence."

For those who are believers in the Almighty, failure becomes easy to handle. Like I believe that whatever happens, happens for our own good. Only, we as yet can't 'see' it. If I fail in one thing that means God wants me not to do that particular thing. I have tried out this permutation and combination and have come out with more than satisfactory results. My own life would have been a tale of failures if I did not accept and acknowledge them on a positive note.

There is panic only when there is a combination of anxiety and fear. I have met people with atychiphobia (abnormal, unwarranted, and persistent fear of failure), who say they can't breathe, feel like dying or go crazy just at the mention of failure. They have made failure their world and can't see beyond the whirlpool.

I have tried to analyze why people tend to panic at failure. Generally, *"Log kya kahenge?"* (what will people say!) is a primary reason. We, Indians, tend to pay more than necessary attention to what people think and talk about us than what we think of ourselves. I have an atychiphobic friend who says she is scared of failure as she thinks failing will take away people's attention and interest in her. She is so unsure about her own capabilities that she does not even attempt anything significant for fear of failure.

Another reason to panic at failure is expectations (read: over-expectations). A friend's brother cut his wrist after "failing" to get a promotion at office. Sounds like a teenager? No, he is a married guy with twins. Thankfully, timely intervention saved his life. But that's not the point. After recovery, when he was asked the reason for the "cowardly" act, he said he did not want to disappoint his kids whom he had promised a trip to Disneyland once he got the much-expected promotion.

The best way to overcome the panic of failure is to own up to it. Admit it, speak about it in public, fearlessly, and also in front of your own self. Once you can count your panic and fear on your fingers, it become easier to vent openly and relieve yourself.

You must practise self-relaxation techniques, believe me they are an immense help. There is yoga and various simple breathing exercises which help you to remain calm and increase your power at controlling panic and anxiety.

Realise what is done cannot be undone.

Above all, we must know that there are certain things in our control and some not in our hands. We must give our 200% dedication and hard work to the part that is in our control and not think too much about what is not. Even in the Bhagavad Gita, Sri Krishna tells the great warrior prince of the Pandavas, Arjun: *"Karmanye vadhikaraste, ma phaleshou kada chana"* (You keep performing your duty without the thought of results because the fruits of your actions are not in your hands).

CHAPTER 9

NEVER QUITTING.
NEVER. EVER

It may be one of the oldest clichés in the world, but like all clichés, it is a core truth: straight and simple, and stands the test of time. This one goes thus: A winner never quits, and a quitter never wins. Truth to say, nothing more needs to be said in this chapter. But it is inspiring to share our thoughts and what we ponder upon when we trot out that old cliché.

It is attributed to Vince Lombardi, a famous American football coach, and we have all heard this at least once in our lives. It comes up in our mind whether we are on the sports field or in the classroom; at work or in our inter-relationships.

A winner will never take a loss or a defeat for an answer. He will plod on, even if unsupported, using the soulful words of the great Indian man of letters, Rabindranath Tagore. In Bengali, it goes like this: *Jodi tor daak shune keu na aashe / Tobe ekla cholo re*, meaning, Even if no one responds to your call / Tread along your path alone. The journey may be tough, challenges and obstacles innumerable, but he will go on, never letting his shoulders droop, never quitting. That's how tough he is, that's what makes him a winner.

On the other hand, a quitter gets jolted by challenges and, not being able to stand up to them, gives up. If he does not have the determination and perseverance to succeed, the inner strength to overcome difficulties, he is never ever going to come up a winner. He will forever remain a quitter, or a 'loser' in contemporary language.

Most of us are not born with talent and skills. But we develop them over time. Whether it is the poor gardener's son, Eknath Solkar, who fought all odds, to become one of India's greatest cricketers, or Sachin Tendulkar known today as the 'god of cricket' the world over, who used each failure as a stepping stone to success, in his own words. It was their passion that got them where they reached.

Similarly, scientists like Issac Newton and Albert Einstein never threw up their hands just because some of their experiments failed. Nor did the remarkable cancer survivors like Indian supermodel Lisa Ray and legendary Hollywood actor Robert Di Niro. And the wonderful example of Helen Keller can never be forgotten. Helen was born with proper hearing and sight abilities, but lost them very early in infancy. It brings tears to my eyes just to glance at her biography, but the world knows how she overcame seemingly insurmountable odds and became one of the greatest -- guess what -- educators of the world!

Nearer home, and as recent as only last year, two names suddenly had the spotlight focussed on them, and they have become legends in their own lifetime. They are both last year's Nobel Peace Prize co-winners: India's Kailash Satyarthi and Pakistan's Malala Yousafzai. The former has dedicated his life for the past 35 years to the eradication of child labour and trafficking, unknown and unsung (till now), and having faced adverse situations and hostility, like beatings and death threats, which would be enough to break any lesser mortal's backbone – literally and metaphorically. Malala, who was shot three times from near point-blank range by the Taliban for being adamant about *not* giving up studies, come what may, survived the bullet in the head by her own sheer will power, and God generously working a miracle. Malala was only 15 then. And today, her advocacy of female education has become an international movement. She has even more resolve to fight back the Taliban and any other who will not allow her to inspire many more children, especially the girl child, to study!

As you can see, to give up midway is easy, but to continue despite challenges is difficult, sometimes "impossible". That is why only winners are remembered and the quitters go to the garden to dig up worms. They live a life of regret, with no motivation or dedication.

When astrophysicist Stephen Hawking wrote *A Brief History of Time*, his publisher had warned him that every mathematical equation in his book would reduce readership by 50 per cent. Hawking under pressure gave in, but included just one: E=mc2. At last count, the book has sold nearly 10 million copies! So, who was right? Who the winner because he stuck it out to whatever extent he could?

It is wise to heed such words as pain being temporary, and the smallest act of surrendering remaining with you through your life. But to end on a sweet note, I must point out the example of champion swimmer Diana Nyad who, in 2013, at last achieved her long-time dream of swimming *without a shark cage* from Havana to Key West -- in her fifth attempt to do so, at the ripe age of 64! "I wanted to teach myself some life lessons at the age of 60," recalled Diana, "and one of them was that you don't give up."

CHAPTER 10

LOST IN TRANSIT? OR, CONNECTING WITH THE SELF?

At some point of later life we want to attain a kind of *sanyaas* (renunciation), a state when good or bad, right or wrong, happiness or sorrow, winning or losing, ceases to make any difference.

Sri Ramakrishna Paramahansa Dev had said it is easier for a sage to pursue a spiritual life than a family man as the former has no distractions, but the latter makes out time to seek the Ultimate Truth even amidst all worldly obstacles.

No matter how successful or unsuccessful we have been in life or how rich or poor we were destined to be in life, it is peace and only peace that remains the primary objective of life at this late stage, which in turn, remains elusive throughout, too.

We never really get to value our own selves. The reason being, we never get to know ourselves as we never found the "time" or motivation to do so. How many of us spend at least ten minutes every day with their own self...and think, get into self-introspection, analyze the happenings outside and inside you?

Vietnamese Zen Buddhist monk Thích Nhất Hạnh had said: "You are what you want to become. Why search anymore? You are a wonderful manifestation. The whole universe has come together to make your existence possible. There is nothing that is not you. The kingdom of God, the Pure Land, *nirvana* (salvation), happiness, and liberation are all you."

No one knows what it feels when one achieves *nirvana*. Gautama Buddha attained *nirvana* and he said: "I reached in experience the *nirvana* which is unborn, unrivalled, secure from attachment, undecaying and unstained. This condition is indeed reached by me which is deep, difficult to see, difficult to understand, tranquil, excellent, beyond the reach of mere logic, subtle, and to be realized only by the wise."

But we never get to really understand an emotion by mere words unless we experience it in person. I believe it comes via practice. And the road to *nirvana* starts with meditation. By meditation, I don't mean leaving all worldly pleasures aside and sitting in a particular position with eyes closed and focusing on imaginary signs and symbols. It's a difficult process for beginners. But, as I mentioned earlier, cutting out from the outside world for some time and spending time with one's own self, concentrating on your deep breathing, and the ups and downs of your pumping heart.

Obviously those who practise the methodical medication get immense benefits. So, slowly when your mind has become accustomed to calming down during that particular time of the day, try "actual" meditation. Here, I would like to quote Buddha again as no mediation is complete without mentioning him and his teachings.

It is a very popular story though. Once Buddha was asked what he has gained from meditation. He said: "Nothing. However, let me tell you what I have lost – anger, anxiety, depression, insecurity, fear of old age and death... peace comes from within. Do not seek it without."

While we are talking about *nirvana*, what exactly did we mean or understand by this term is debatable. There are different views about it, though I would like to describe *nirvana* as a state that frees us from all that binds us or we cling to in life.

I was discussing *nirvana* the other day when an old friend sarcastically said: "You want to be a *grihasth-sanyaasi* (turn a sage while enjoying family life)? Then, just detach yourself from all desires." It is not about giving away your assets -- money and other valuables -- to charity or some other person.

Long back, I met a sage in Vrindavan who was also a foodie. When I asked him what made him so attached to *pet puja* (stomach or hunger worship), he replied: "*Bhojan ke bina bhajan nahin hota hai*" (you cannot sing carols to God on an empty stomach). Try meditating after starving yourself the whole day and you will understand.

A mental discipline is always required when you want to turn detached to family woes and happiness. And this discipline does not come in one day. The value has to be instilled since childhood. But that does not mean that adults or elders are not "qualified" for *nirvana*. To begin with, try to make a schedule for everything and try to maintain that. Sleep, wake up, eat, drink, relax, meditate and even chat with friends at a definite time every day. You are sure to fail in keeping up with your commitment during the initial days, but do not give up hope and stick to the regime. Once your body gets a definite biological clock to maintain and respond to, it will automatically start emitting a positive vibration for the mind.

Also, eating right has positive effects on the body and mind. When we start eating less junk food and more nutrious stuff, the body starts healing itself. Our food, in a major way, influences our mood. It is now scientifically proved that changes in our diet bring chemical as well as psychological changes in our brain structure.

Once the body is at peace, the mind also calms down and it helps in regularising the process of meditation. The effects of meditation cannot be undermined as the quality of "me" time it gives us surpasses all other distractions.

Even in the Bhagavad Gita, it is mentioned: "*Yunjann evam sadatmanam yogi vigata-kalmasah sukhena brahma-samsparsam atyantam sukham asnute*", meaning: By doing yoga, one can remain in constant touch with the Self and lose all grossness.

Also, another thing that will help you detach yourself from your family and outer world is by letting go. Learn to let go of things that affect your peace of mind. You need not shout the roof down when a neighbour by mistake throws garbage into your backyard. Sweeping it with a broom and keeping your space clean will not hamper your self-respect.

And, try to avoid "toxic" people who in no way contribute to your life other than negatively. Negative energy around you can spoil your own cleansed aura. You don't have to show them the door every time they come to your place, but surely you can find an excuse to avoid them.

Above all, remember happiness is what is beating inside you.

As Roman Emperor and Stoic philosopher Marcus Aurelius said: "Very little is needed to make a happy life; it is all within yourself, in your way of thinking."

CHAPTER 11

GIVING...AND FORGIVING

After you have achieved your goals and lived your dreams, what next? And what if you still need to gather yourself and your little savings "for the future"; what then? It brings to mind a little tale I was hearing the other day on television. The spiritual guru referred to the example of a beggar woman who donated a lakh (0.1 million) of rupees to the temple before which she begged for decades. This was reported in the media. When asked how she managed to do that, she explained that she had survived and sustained herself by begging before that temple. So, wasn't it fair that she set aside a few coins or rupees for the temple? She ended up with a lakh of rupees which she donated to the temple which had given her that, and more. Sure, it must have pinched the old beggar lady quite a bit, but what a spirit of giving! What an act of prayer, I would say!

When it comes to giving, the classic statement of Mother Teresa flashes in the mind of almost everybody. "Give," Mother Teresa famously said, "but give until it hurts." How can anyone put it better than that? On another occasion, Mother had elaborated, "It's not how much we give but how much love we put into giving." *That* is the real point.

How true it is in life. My mother used to say, "One should always donate or contribute to the poor and unfortunate because it multiplies and comes back to you in your difficult times."

When your hair turns grey, and you grow wiser, you realize that you have two hands. Most believe it has always been for *Ek haath de aur ek haath le*, meaning, give by one hand and take back by the other. But that is only a business deal, not a deal of love and compassion. The fact is that one hand is for helping yourself and the other for helping the less blessed, the children of a lesser god. Remember, Anne Frank said, "No one has ever become poor by giving."

Frankly, this uplifting lyric from the Bollywood film of yore, *Badal*, sung by Manna De, keeps me going -- and giving. *Apne liye / Jiye to kya jiye / Tu jee, ay dil / Zamaane ke liye* (Living for yourself / Is no living at all / Live, dear self / For the world at large)... It has become a motivating song for me every morning.

Of course, there will always remain unfulfilled dreams otherwise you have reached a stage of vegetation. Even if you think you have, you will think of things that you failed to achieve despite your best efforts, despite never quitting. And you will have regrets, lingering regrets. In modern language they speak of that as 'unnecessary baggage'.

In this journey of life, as most hikers, adventure seekers and airlines advise, travel light. The first thing in order to travel light is to carry only the bare essentials and throw out the rest from your bags. They all seem like things you just can't do without. But when you think rationally you will learn how to make decisions cleverly and realistically.

In earlier decades, at least in this great subcontinent, train journeys were very long and dusty with coal flying in your face from the steam locomotives, no matter what preventive measures you took. It necessitated carrying heavy bedrolls, and a trunk full of clothes and bedsheets and food to last some 48 hours, which were more necessary during the journey than when you reached your destination.

Have things changed as the years and decades have rolled past? Of course! To the extent that the younger generation cannot fathom the romance of train journeys in their air conditioned coaches of super express trains with black tinted window panes. The air conditioned cocoons which not only keep prying eyes at bay, but also close your own vision of the glorious world outside. The high-tech electric trains move so smoothly that you can never hear the rhythmic run on the rails, which was great music to our ears in childhood. Sad to say, even if you could hear those marvellous beats of the steel wheels, you would probably be with your headphones or earphones on and listening to more worldly music or perhaps chatting on your smartphones! And you can even recharge your batteries in the coupe itself!

But the good thing is, among other positive things, that we can really travel light now. Almost as light as when you travel by flight. It has added convenient and comfortable travel, and even by train you have cut down on your travel time by almost half. Simply owing to technical and technological advancement through the decades. Which has, in turn, helped you leave that heavy baggage behind, in more senses than one!

It's the same when you decide to leave that baggage behind, baggage that is weighing you down and making you drag your feet through life. And move on, to your own advantage, to say the least. This very thought of travelling light in life must be making you feel that you are sailing through life with the moist winds whistling through your hair. Wouldn't you rather have this life?

You must have surely noticed that the extension of 'giving' seems to be 'forgiving'. Or, if you look at it the other way about, part of the word 'forgiving' is 'giving'. So both giving and forgiving go hand-in-hand.

The other face of giving or charity or generosity is forgiving. How? This is how. When you forgive, you are being generous, are you not? No matter who was at fault, you sincerely want to put all that negativity away in the past. You are not only being generous to the other party, but actually being more than generous to yourself. You gain nothing by nursing that hurt, that humiliation, that attack on your body and soul. By nursing that grievance you are only allowing the wound to fester. And that wound is on your *own* body and soul. So who are you doing an act of generosity by forgiving? Think. There is only one answer.

Yourself. The sooner you press the Delete button on the past hurt, humiliation, grievances, the better for *you*.

Forgiveness is not true compassion. What is to be compassionate? Please find out for yourself. Think it out, whether a mind that is hurt can ever forgive? Can a mind that is capable of being hurt ever forgive? And can such a mind, which is capable of being hurt, be compassionate?

The mind is not conscious of itself as being compassionate, as loving. But the moment you forgive consciously, the mind is strengthening at its own centre, its own hurt. The point I am trying to make is that the mind which *consciously* forgives can never actually forgive, it does not know real forgiveness. It forgives in order not to be further hurt, or keep vengeance in cold storage for the moment. Forgiveness must be compassionate, not conscious, in other words.

So as long as there is conscious cultivation of any particular influence, any particular virtue, there can be no love, there can be no compassion, because love and compassion are not the result of conscious effort.

There is this other factor. In forgiving, you are not only doing yourself a huge favour, you are also sending out positive energy to the other. That is real charity, real generosity. It makes you grow as a person, helps cutting out negative energy and emanating positive energy instead. The world looks sunny again! And you can just move on, having done yourself a huge favour, and put in effort and positivity into your next and other ventures, aims and goals.

It's very simple if you think about it. By forgiving, you are not obliged to kiss and make up, or send them multiple smileys on Facebook or SMSes. But at least you can unshackle the rocks on your feet, the rocks of regret and rancour, that are weighing down your wings and disabling you from taking flight. Even the Holy Bible states, "They who forgive most shall be most forgiven."

When we pray, there are usually two things we beg for: God, save me from evil; God, forgive me my sins. So -- forgive me for asking -- why can't *we* forgive the other's sins? Isn't that just fair before we beg God for forgiveness?

After all, Mahatma Gandhi whom India reveres as the Father of the Nation, unshaken in his faith in humanity in the midst of historical bloody riots, had said, "An eye for an eye only ends up making the whole world blind."

On a lighter and pithy note, however, no one can match Oscar Wilde. "Always forgive your enemies; nothing annoys them so much." That should be sufficient reason for most of us to forgive!

CHAPTER 12

FINAL WORDS: EVERY MOMENT OF LIFE IS A CELEBRATION

It's one life...even if you believe in reincarnation, it makes no sense because you as YOU won't remember anything. Life is God's best gift to mankind and we must cherish every moment of it.

I love a quote by American actress and media magnate Oprah Winfrey, where she says: "The more you praise and celebrate your life, the more there is in life to celebrate."

We are always in a hurry, and in the hurry of earning bread-and-butter, in the hurry of perfecting our performances in the various roles that we play daily, we overlook and neglect the most beautiful thing that happened to us, and that is life. However, we tend to forget that with every passing second we are getting closer to death and life is being "spent" and not "lived". No one, rich or poor, powerful or weak, successful or a failure, is immortal. My professor in college said once, and it has stuck in my mind ever since, that life comes along with death, they don't come separately. It is very much like a *chandan ka pedh* (sandal tree) and a *saanp* (snake) which will always dwell there. Life is inevitable, so is death. End of debate.

Hence, it is very necessary to make it a habit to celebrate life every day and every moment with even the smallest of simple joys. If you have a target at your workplace and family to meet up, make a target on enjoyment and celebration of life as well.

Every day, no matter how busy I am, I make it a point to relish every meal, every morsel I have. Being a foodie, the inclination towards delicacies comes naturally to me. But on second thoughts, what is the primary purpose of our running around? To ensure me and my family do not starve. I consider my meals as treats provided by the Almighty and hence my eyes automatically close with sheer pleasure every time I take a bite of any well-made food item. That in true manner explains gluttony when they say, I don't eat to live, but I live to eat. Stretched further, that is pure gluttony, not the real meaning of enjoying every moment in life, every morsel the Almighty provides you.

Simple joys in life can be anything ranging from playing with your pet to going for a long walk with ice-cream or tea breaks in between to reading a good book to listening to the rain drops to admiring a good piece of art or music. Trust me, life never offers a single moment of boredom, it is we who infect it with all negativities.

Celebration of life is incomplete without drawing your dear ones into it. Human beings are by nature emotional creatures. We want to share everything -- our joys, our sorrows, our guilt, our pride, good, bad, ugly, just about everything with people around us. So, I have realised that reconnecting with a friend or relative, with whom you have lost touch for ages, does wonders.

Just think about it, there was a friend in college with whom you broke up on a very bitter note. But obviously you could not wipe out the good memories you two shared. Life took its own course and you moved on. You are now 63 with a still noisy yet doting wife, grandchildren and pension. But there is still an aching of the past. You still have a faded photo of hers in that drawer which no one is allowed to touch, and wish you could see her once before you died. You even fantasised how she would be looking now -- whether she dyes her hair or keeps it salt-and-pepper, whether she has got fatter or thinner, whether her husband is still alive, and the like.

One day, your eldest grandson teaches you Facebooking and opens an account of yours on the social media. And then, one lazy afternoon, while surfing on Facebook, you casually type her name, and bingo! She is right there. You send a friend request and she accepts. How will you define that moment of sheer joy and "teenage" happiness that still found a way to your heart? That very moment you feel like celebrating your life and thanking your luck that you are still alive to experience this.

Coming to another *mantra* (a supposedly holy chant) for celebrating life, when was the last time you clicked yourself? I am not talking about selfies but actual portfolio kind of thing? Even if you are not a camera-friendly person, try getting yourself photographed in various poses by a professional photographer. Photo sessions give a great boost to your ego. If you don't believe me, ask Bollywood diva Rekha, for one!

At times it is a great feeling doing nothing and simply lying on the couch or bed, spreading yourself out, and listening to your favourite music, eyes closed, or watching a film with a popcorn bowl. Try to push this into your Sunday regime and see how refreshed you feel about life.

Another thing that we generally avoid doing in our entire lifetime is to indulge in what we consider as luxury. Suppose you fancy travelling in AC buses but most of the time you avoid boarding one to save a few bucks which, when accumulated for a couple of days, can be used to pay off for a kilogramme of wheat flour. We always do that. But at times, it's okay to do what you want. It's not a crime to get that new smartphone for yourself instead of gifting it to your son. He can have his by saving his pocket money, if he really wants to.

Also, how often do you watch the sunrise and the sunset? Don't have the time, right? Well, if there is a will, there is a way. Try sitting all by yourself and watching the magic of nature. There is no balm more soothing than the beauty of nature. If you have green fingers, you can also try gardening. It's a great feeling to see the plants grow, the buds opening to become flowers, butterflies enhancing the variant colours at your garden.

You cannot celebrate life without pampering the child in you. Even at this age, I love to play the games I enjoyed as a child, and some of my neighbouring kids join me too in a game of snakes and ladders, marbles or carom. I still love solving crossword puzzles during the afternoons, they are great fun and stimulate my mind with nostalgia. There is a friend who still goes to the park and sits at the swings late evening after the children have gone home.

If you have a wish and that wish is okay for your pocket, fulfil that, no matter how weird it may seem... Days before his death, my grandfather bought himself a bright red umbrella. When I expressed my astonishment, he said while in school, he used to fancy a girl, not because she was beautiful but because, he thought, she had the most beautiful red umbrella in the world! He always wanted to have that umbrella, but in vain. So, now at the ripe age of 91, he decided to give his wish one last shot.

Like him, celebrate life! Because life itself is a celebration. Every moment of it.

Epilogue

When I completed my Higher Secondary in school, I applied for a job with Calcutta Medical & Research Institute (CMRI). After an anxious wait of about two weeks, I visited their HR office, wanting to impress upon them how desperately I needed the job.

I knew that it was not the proper thing to do, especially when I had only just passed out of school. But to my utter surprise, two days later I got a call asking me to meet the HR head.

The HR officer asked me, "How sure are you of getting this job?" I replied, "Sir, I am aware that I may not be the most competent candidate, or even eligible, but this job is very important to me. As important to me as my very life."

Under my breath, I added, "I want to support my studies and my ego as well."

The instant retort was, "What do you mean by your ego?"

"No, no, Sir," I fumbled. "This is my first application for this first job and I am pretty sure that I will give my 100 per cent." The officer's curiosity was aroused and he further enquired why I wasn't going in for further education since Higher Secondary was not even graduation.

"No, Sir, I mean, I want to complete my graduation, but I am not sure that my parents can afford my education at this stage. We are four siblings and I have decided to support my own education whether you offer this job or not."

Hearing my firm reply and seeing my body language, the HR head of CMRI asked me to wait outside his office. Within an hour and a half, I had clinched it! A dream had come true. Didn't that great spiritual scholar Swami Vivekananda talk of singleminded passion and a sharp focus on what you really want? "Take up one idea. Make that one idea your life -- think of it, dream of it, live on that idea," he said. And never even *think* of giving up. That is the only key to success.

I was bitten by the bug of writing this book about ten years ago. I was inspired to write it, I lived with that idea every day. I knew I had very many ideas, I had travelled a long way in life, like the illustrious American President Abraham Lincoln almost, from the log cabin to the White House! At least, I felt so, though it may sound immodest.

I have seen poverty, but never let it get me down even in childhood. I have, by the grace of God, gone from strength to strength and wallowed in every moment of it; the bad times and the good times.

I wanted now to share my life experiences so that others like my dear readers could also feel inspired. The book has seen fruition now.

Life as a celebration never ceases to throw up a new shining example every minute of the day and night. Even at the final stage of proof reading of this book, *Life is a Celebration*, I learnt that this leading modern Bengali singer, the very versatile Anasua Choudhury was returning to singing accompanied by a surge of emotions.

You might wonder what I mean by "returning". Return from where? After how long?

The lady was laid low by the cruel hand of Fate some four years ago. A long-time diabetic, she was suddenly struck by paralysis and could no longer sing -- her lifeblood and passion. But God not only gave Anasua Choudhury fierce courage and will power, but also a set of doting fans and wellwishers, not to speak of self-effacing and supportive family members especially husband.

Even while I was busy with the last minute touches to this book, this joyous news came by. We will soon hear her dulcet voice again, surging with the same sonorous power. And someone has already been inspired to make a documentary on her!

Of course, there is a legion of such amazing people. These examples, closer home, serve to illustrate the main point I am trying to make, which is:

This is the power of our dream, the passion, focus and sheer determination. And I repeat: Never Quitting. Never. Ever.

P.S. It is pleasing to find an echo of my feelings in an illustrator's works. This illustrator is dear friend and eminent illustrator Sanjib Chaudhuri. In the following pages, you will find some of his fine sketches. As in any art, I leave you to discover your own interpretations of life as a celebration in everyday life.

HOTEL
TERMA LINCA
THIMPU
25.12.2011

29.10.2012

SANJB JAN 2011

একটি উষ্ণতার দিনরাত

।রাত।

এখন এই সুখের রাতে,
আরেকটি দেহের উষ্ণতার আরামে,
ওর মা'কে মনে পড়ছে।

।দিন।

শীতের আবছা সকাল।
ঠাকুরিয়া ব্রীজের ওপরে উপচে পড়া ভ্যাটটার দিকে
নির্লজ্জের মত ছুটছে,
সাত সাতটি সদ্যজাতের মা,
নিজের না জুটুক, ওদের ক্ষিদে ত পায়েই।

কর্পোরেশনের রাক্ষস লরীটা
কুয়াশায় চোখ জ্বেলে, দাঁত বের করে ছুটে আসছে।
ক্ষিদের আগুন ছুটছে তারও আগে।
রাক্ষসের ক্ষিদে মেটার আগেই খুঁজে নিতে হবে,
যদি কিছু খুঁজে পাওয়া যায়।

*****

এক টুকরো ক্ষীণ, দীর্ঘ, অসমাপ্ত স্বর।
মা'র গলায় এমন ডাক ওর অচেনা।
রাক্ষসের নখর পায়ের তলায় লেপ্টে আছে
উষ্ণ রক্তে ভেজা শরীর কালো পীচ ঢালা রাস্তায়।
মা'র শুকনো বাদামী রং হঠাৎ কেমন গোলাপী।

জীবনের শেষ পাওনা মেটায় সাত সকালের অফিস যাত্রী।
নাকে রুমাল চেপে একরাশ বিরক্তি।